Kingdom Airways
The Quick Sketch Collection

Stephen Deal

Tried & Tested

Nimbus Press

Copyright

We are mainly interested in providing resources for churches that want to use drama in worship, in bible study and in evangelism, and for Amateur Dramatic Groups. You are free to perform any of our plays and sketches and do not need permission but we would appreciate receiving news of any productions. **All our books are protected by copyright and so we ask that you buy copies for each actor when you perform the dramas.** We hope that you will find them useful for the work of the Kingdom.

Fees for performances by professional companies will be subject to negotiation.

Published by Nimbus Press,
18 Guilford Road, Leicester LE2 2RB.
Email: publisher@nimbuspress.demon.co.uk
Cover illustration by Polly Deal.

Copyright © Stephen Deal, 2000.

British Library Cataloguing in Publication
Data available

ISBN 1 874424 62 4

Printed in Great Britain by Saville Press
Illiffe House, Illiffe Avenue, Oadby,
Leicester, LE2 5LS, England.

Contents

Acknowledgements

The material in this book was written over a period of many years. Countless people came up with ideas and bits of ideas for sketches, or encouraged me to try this and that, this way or that way. Thanks to you all. I would particularly like to thank Kevin Daniel, Stephanie Reese, David Newell, Karen Fox-Williams, Julian Carr and Caroline Goodwin who toured the country performing my material at various times between 1985 and 1994 as Stripes Theatre Company. I'd also like to thank Kate Strafford and John Talbot for their contribution to the work of the Quick Sketch Company over recent years.

In addition I'd like to take this opportunity to thank Rob Frost for his support over the years. If he hadn't started to use us back in 1986 things would have been very different indeed.

And finally, I'd be endangering my life if I didn't thank Polly Deal for … well just about everything. Polly acts in my sketches, illustrates my book covers and provides constant love and attention to her temperamental, ego-centric husband. Marrying her was quite simply the best idea I've ever had. Thanks Polly.

Introduction

Welcome to Kingdom Airways, my second selection of sketches from the Quick Sketch Collection. Presumably the very fact that you are reading this means you have some interest in Christian drama (or that you are a close friend or relative of mine and have received this book as a cheap birthday present). My own interest in Christian drama goes way back to the summer of 1984 to when I spent a lifetime one weekend at the Greenbelt festival. Most of the group I was with spent hours watching distant specks on a faraway stage sing songs about how absolutely lovely it is to be a Christian. Meanwhile, a friend and I discovered the altogether more immediate (and because it was in a tent, warmer and dryer) experience of live Christian theatre. Some of what we watched was fast, clever and innovative, other shows were cringingly embarrassing. My friend and I said, "We can do that." and promptly formed our own drama group. We had no training and only a little experience picked up along the way via Christian Drama Company productions at college. Our first performances were in Student Union bars, often with beer being offered at less than half price. It was a steep learning curve. At times we added our own new chapters to the book on cringing embarrassment but eventually experience began to teach us what worked and how to pack up and exit a building quickly when it didn't.

Starting a drama group need not be difficult but certain considerations do need to be thought about right at the outset. Find people who are prepared to commit time and energy to the project. Lots of people fancy themselves as actors but are unprepared to spend time learning lines and rehearsing. Be realistic about the projects you undertake. There is little point in taking on a show if the script requires twenty men on camels to enter stage right in a sand storm, when you've a group of four, and the only area to perform in is between the front pew and the communion rail. Fortunately hardly any of the sketches in this collection require a camel or, indeed, any other beast of burden.

You should be sensitive to the audience you are playing to, especially while you are building a reputation. I know someone who attended a little rural church one Christmas where the youth group had been given a slot to do their own version of a Nativity play. Mary came on in fishnet stockings and the shepherds were portrayed as punk rockers complete with green hair and plastic bin-bag outfits. The elderly congregation watched open-mouthed as the birth of our saviour was translated into an urban fable. Man will have colonised Mars before the vicar lets drama into that church again. If you are starting out go for material that has been tried and tested in front of an audience (rather like the material in this book).

And finally, a little while ago I was greeted warmly by someone at a conference whom I did not recognise. My blank look alerted this person to the fact that I had no memory of her and she reminded me of the fact that I had visited her church with my theatre company. My face must have shifted from blank to puzzled. She then reminisced about one sketch in particular. She described the characters and the situation. She even recalled snatches of the dialogue and several of the jokes, including the punchline. It was little wonder I did not remember the visit; for the sketch described went out of the company's repertoire over ten years earlier. Whatever else it is, drama is memorable. I hope this book provides you with suitable material for you and your group to use but remember it's your performance that will make a lasting impact on your audience. Good luck.

Kingdom Airways

Characters
Sabrina
Dominic

Bible Background
Matthew 19. 23-31

Sabrina and Dominic are flight attendants on a plane about to depart. Sabrina reads the instructions while Dominic demonstrates them.

Sabrina   Hello and welcome to Kingdom Airways - the service that takes you to paradise. My name is Sabrina and I'll be your flight attendant for the duration of your journey. Now, if you'll pay attention to my colleague Dominic for just one moment, he will demonstrate the safety procedures. Thank you.

A useful guide to the Kingdom can be found tucked into a pocket on the back of the pew in front of you. We suggest you familiarise yourself with the details contained therein because it does include vital instructions regarding entry requirements into our destination. Also you will find a complimentary bag of sweets with particularly rustly wrappers to give relief during take off, landing and the sermon.

In the unlikely event of an emergency please take up crash positions, thus.

Dominic takes up a position of fervent prayer.

In the even more unlikely event of a forced landing into the sea please pull on your life jacket thus. Inflate by blowing thus. And attract attention to yourself by blowing on your whistle thus. Unless you are in a praise band in which case you should play 'Nearer My God to Thee' as loudly as you can. Those of you with hassocks under your seats may use them as a flotation device. Those of you who oppose adult baptism may have to rethink your position.

The Evangelical Churches will be sitting in the comfy seats whilst the rest of you sit on wooden pews. Anglicans will also have to sit behind a pillar.

For your comfort the front section of this aircraft has been designated a non-smoking area. Anglo-Catholics will have to sit at the back.

If you wish to attract the attention of a flight attendant please raise your hand - except for the charismatics who have their hands up already - you should lower yours. Refreshments will be served but I'm afraid the Methodists can only have the Hymn Sandwich.

Should the plane begin to shake violently then please do not worry. We may be experiencing turbulence or possibly a return of the 'Toronto blessing'.

May we remind all passengers that all extraneous theology should be stored in the compartments above their seats. Not for the first time will it go over people's heads.

We realise the plane has been waiting on the runway for sometime now. The captain says we're still waiting for clearance for take off to our final destination. We'd like to give you a precise time of departure but, "... of that day and hour knoweth no man, not even the angels in heaven."

When we do finally arrive in the Kingdom may we remind passengers that when it comes to exiting the plane that the many who are in first class shall be last. Passengers must disembark via the exits provided. These are the only possible routes into the Kingdom of God. They are not located here and here but are located here and here.

Dominic indicates exits immediately on his left and right. He is left in a cruciform position.

Thank you for travelling with us. Have a good journey!
END

The Swap Shop

Characters
Beverly
Customer

Bible Background
Exodus 20.1-17

Beverly stands behind a customer services counter. A customer approaches.

Beverly   Next please. Welcome to customer services. My name is Beverly. How may I be of assistance?

Cust.   It's about these.

The customer places two bags which contain stone tablets on the counter.

Beverly   May I be so forward as to enquire as to the contents of these bags?

Cust.   Tablets.

Beverly   In that case may I direct you in the direction of the pharmacy where they specialise in all manner of tablets?

Cust.   These are stone tablets.

Beverly   That must make them very difficult to swallow.

Cust.   These are stone tablets with the Ten Commandments written on them.

Beverly   Lovely. And how may I be of service to you?

Cust.   I don't like them.

Beverly	Oh dear. Are they broken?
Cust.	Frequently.
Beverly	I mean is there a fault in the product?
Cust.	They're too hard.
Beverly	Well they are made of stone.
Cust.	Not the tablets, the commandments. The commandments are too hard.
Beverly	I see.
Cust.	I want my money back.
Beverly	Do you have a receipt?
Cust.	No. They were a sort of gift. A man came down out of the mountains and gave them to us.
Beverly	That was nice of him.
Cust.	But I don't like them. I'd prefer the cash.
Beverly	Well that does present me with a bit of a problem. I am unable to give cash refunds without evidence of purchase. To whit, a receipt.
Cust.	Does that mean I'm stuck with them?
Beverly	I suppose we could offer to exchange them.
Cust.	What can I get for them?
Beverly	How about a handful of proverbs? You know the kind of thing. You can lead a horse to water but you can't make him drink. A stitch in time saves nine. I could let you have ten of those instead.

Cust.	I don't know. What else is there?
Beverly	I could offer you maxims, aphorisms, adages, clichés, axioms or homilies.
Cust.	They sound exciting. Can I swap my Ten Commandments for ten of those?
Beverly	Certainly Sir, if that's what you really want.
Cust.	Of course it's what I really want. Have you seen the Ten Commandments?
Beverly	Oh yes. I'm a big fan of Charlton Heston.
Cust.	No, I mean have you read the Ten Commandments?
Beverly	Well, we did do them in Sunday School. They seemed perfectly fair to me then.
Cust.	Fair? I am the Lord your God, who brought you out of the land of Egypt, out of the house of bondage. You shall have no other gods before me.
Beverly	So?
Cust.	That's restrictive practices, that is.
Beverly	Is it? Oh. I thought it was God saying, "I've set you free. If you worship other gods you might end up as a slave again."
Cust.	What about not making graven images, hey? Does that mean we shouldn't draw any pictures?
Beverly	I think it says we shouldn't worship them.
Cust.	Who would be so stupid as to worship a graven image? A picture? Look, are you sure I can't get a cash refund? After all,

money's what it's all about these days. Lovely crisp fivers and shiny coins.

Beverly I'm sorry, Sir. It's company policy.

Cust. Well it's a silly policy, like the rest of the commandments are silly. Don't do this and don't do that.

Beverly Don't swear, murder, steal, commit adultery, covet or lie. Make sure you have time to rest and respect your parents. They sound rather good to me. Are you sure you want to exchange them?

Cust. Yes. I'd like some of those other things.

Beverly What? The maxims, aphorisms, adages, clichés, axioms or homilies? Which would you like?

Cust. Can I have a selection?

Beverly Just so I'm clear, you want to swap the Ten Commandments for a mixture of other rules and sayings?

Cust. Yes.

Beverly Like going to the pick 'n' mix counter in a sweet shop.

Cust. How do you mean?

Beverly Well, in my experience, when given lots of choice with no restrictions people tend to only choose what they like.

Cust. Which is?

Beverly Lots of sweetness, nothing sticky, soft in the centre and absolutely nothing worth getting your teeth into. Next please.

END

Mind Your Mannas

Characters
Ben
Zara
Zack

Bible Background
'The Israelites all complained ...' Exodus 16

Zara   Supper's ready!

Ben   Coming, mum.

Zara   Have you seen your father?

Ben   He was talking to Moses and Aaron over by their tent.

Zara   Was he really just talking?

Ben   Well no, he was shouting and stamping his feet a lot actually.

Zara   I don't know what good he thinks it'll do moaning on at them. It's God who'll decide if we're ever to leave this wilderness.

Zack comes storming in.

Zack   I don't believe it. I really do not believe it.

Zara   Good evening dear.

Zack   They haven't got a clue.

Zara   Really dear? A clue about what?

Zack   About leadership. About good government. Traipsing around in a sun-baked desert is no way to promote sustained economic growth.

Zara	What did Moses say?
Zack	Oh, the usual stuff about following the Lord our God into a promised land.
Zara	Well God has looked after us pretty well up to now.
Zack	Well yes, granted he has manifested himself now and then with the odd miracle and tablet of stone, but a pillar of dust by day and of fire by night is no substitute for a carefully formulated mission statement. What's for supper?
Zara	Take a wild guess.
Zack	Oh please tell me it's roast partridge in a light orange sauce with broccoli and sautéed potatoes.
Zara	You wouldn't want me to lie to you, would you?
Ben	Is it manna?
Zara	Yes.
Ben	Yummy!
Zack	It's always manna. Manna fried, manna boiled, manna roasted.
Ben	I like manna.
Zack	Manna grilled, manna baked, manna al dente.
Zara	It's all there is.
Zack	I'm sick of it. I'm sick of everything. I want to go back to Egypt.
Zara	But we didn't have our freedom in Egypt.
Zack	Oh right. And what's so great about freedom? Freedom to get sunburn from the desert sun, freedom to get blisters from

walking on the desert sand, freedom to get stung by all manner of poisonous creepy-crawlies that hide in the desert.

Zara I warned you to check your underwear before putting it on.

Zack At least in Egypt we knew where we were.

Ben What was Egypt like, dad?

Zack It was a wonderful place, son. Full of pyramids. It had glorious architecture and beautiful temples. There was full employment and we were happy there.

Zara You moaned the whole time!

Zack I didn't!

Zara You did! You said that the temples were gaudy and tasteless and blasphemous. You even complained that the pyramids were too sharp to sit on. You demanded somebody do something about the working conditions and above all you moaned about not having your freedom.

Zack Well yes, but now I realise that slavery and back-breaking labour are preferable to another meal of manna!

Zara You are never satisfied, that's your problem. Moan, moan, moan. God delivers you out of slavery and all you can do is whinge about how miserable everything is. Do you remember what you said when Moses held out his arms and the Red Sea parted before our very eyes.

Zack No.

Zara You said, "That was a perfectly good bit of ocean and he's gone and broken it."

Zack I thought we'd get into trouble.

Zara	And when Moses came down from the mountain carrying the Ten Commandments, what did you say?
Zack	I can't remember.
Zara	You said, "Did he have to write them on stone tablets. Didn't he realise how heavy that would make them to lug around the wilderness."
Zack	I'm just sick of this endless wandering. On and on we go. Didn't anyone think to pack a map?
Ben	Where are we headed?
Zara	To a land of milk and honey.
Zack	Hurrah! Two more items on the menu.
Ben	I wonder when we'll get there. I'm going to see if I can find out
Zara	We'll get there when God wants us to get there.
Zack	I just hope it's soon.
Zara	Didn't you ask Moses and Aaron if they know?
Zack	They told me not to worry. They said the people of God aren't meant to just stand still and stagnate.
Zara	Well I expect we'll be there any day now.
Zack	I doubt it. We're going to go on and on forever. After all we've been travelling for thirty-nine years, three hundred and sixty-four days now. If we get there anytime soon, I'll eat my hat.
Ben	Dad! Dad! I've just seen the promised land. It's across that river.
Zack	*(Looking at hat)* Oh well, at least it makes a change from manna. END

Worn To Be King

Characters
Gasper
Tammy
Zara

Bible Background
Matthew 2. 1-12

Gasper (a wise man / king) is preparing to go out. The clothes he wears are particularly garish. Zara, his wife, and Tammy, his daughter, watch him getting ready.

Gasper   Have you seen my crown, Zara?

Zara   I expect it's where you left it, Gasper.

Gasper   Yes, but where is it?

Zara   Lying on the floor of the bathroom waiting for me to pick it up, I expect.

Gasper   Can you have a look?

Tammy   Aw dad, you're not going out wearing your crown are you?

Gasper   Yes.

Tammy   You're so embarrassing, you are.

Zara   Your father can hardly go out kinging without his crown can he? People won't know what he his.

Tammy   Dressed the way he dresses people'll know exactly what he his.

Gasper   Show some respect young lady.

Zara   Where are you going this time?

Gasper   I'm just meeting up with a couple of the lads. We've spotted this star and we thought we'd check it out.

Zara   That's nice dear. Will you be taking the camel?

Gasper   Yes.

Zara   Well you'll need to stop at the oasis and fill it up. I went shopping earlier. Bought some lovely frankincense.

Tammy   What's so special about this star?

Gasper   Melchior reckons it signifies the birth of a new King.

Zara   Oh, lovely. Where do you think he's been born?

Gasper   According to our charts, somewhere in Israel.

Zara   Israel! You be careful if you're going that way.

Gasper   Why? What's so dangerous about Israel?

Tammy   They probably have fashion police. I expect it's an offence to wear loud clothes in a built-up area.

Gasper   Shall I wear my red cloak or my green one?

Tammy   Try an invisible one.

Zara   Isn't Israel where that Herod is king?

Gasper   I think so.

Zara   He's supposed to be a real bully. You stay clear of him. I know what you're like when you get together with Melchior and Balthazar.

Gasper   We're just going to pop over and pay our respects to the new King.

Zara   Just be careful. He's a nasty piece of work that Herod.

Gasper   All we'll do is nip in and ask for directions. Where's the harm in that?

Tammy   If you're looking for a new King surely all you have to do is look for a big royal palace and follow the trail of servants bearing piles of freshly laundered nappies.

Gasper   According to Melchior it may be a bit more complicated than that. For some reason straw seems to feature rather heavily in the calculations.

Tammy   Straw?

Gasper   You know, the stuff they feed animals with.

Zara   How strange.

Gasper   That's not the half of it. When we did all the mathematics to find out where the child would be King the answer kept coming out as everywhere.

Tammy   I expect you've just misplaced a decimal point or two. The King of the Universe is hardly going to be born in a backwater like Israel.

Gasper   I expect you're right. Well I must be off. Do I look suitably kingly?

Zara   You look lovely.

Tammy   Just don't tell anyone you're my dad.

Zara   If I were you I'd pick up a present for the baby on your way. It's only being polite.

Gasper   Bye then.

EXIT Gasper

Zara I bet he forgets. Oh bother.

Tammy What?

Zara I forgot to unload the frankincense from the camel.

END

John the Symbolic Washer of Dirty People

Characters
Jason
John

Bible Background
John 1.1-8, 19-23

John stands or sits on a rock or chair.

Jason John, John, John. What are we to do with you? No, don't say anything, I'm thinking. The muse is upon me. Thank goodness someone saw fit to call me in. We could have had a disaster on our hands.

Jason refers to some notes he has on a clipboard.

It says here you are a prophet. What does that entail? No don't tell me it doesn't matter. All that I need to know is that you are a public figure with an image problem. And as a professional Image Consultant let me tell you image is everything.

Let us start with the name shall we. Hmm ... John. That's good. Simple, straight-forward, honest. The John part's great, we'll keep it. I'm a little more worried about the Baptist bit. John the Baptist. It has a ring to it I'll give you that. John the Baptist. My worry is that not everyone will know what a Baptist is. Perhaps we should consider John the Symbolic Washer of Dirty People? ... No? Never mind, we'll come back to that.

Moving on. John, I like you. I like you a lot. You're an interesting man. Unique. Now, sometimes unique is good and sometimes it's a distraction. Frankly in your case it's not good. It's a matter of consumer brand affiliation. The public can't relate to a man dressed in camel hair. I suggest we put you in to a costume that befits your status. I see silk, I see blue, I see purple. I want your clothes to shout, "Look at me! I'm important". At the moment they shout, "Look at me! I need a boutique".

I think we need to lose the beard. Perhaps we should move to a goatee? What do you think? No, don't say anything, I can tell you love it. I'll organise a stylist.

Refers to notes

Now, let's see ... It says here you stand in a river up to your waist while you do your thing. Now, John, do we need the water? No, no, think about it. You've got good legs and people just can't see them. Also I think this business of you pouring water over people needs a rethink. You may be liable if someone catches a cold. The last thing we need is a law suit. What about if you stood by the side of the river and asked people to think wet thoughts. Wouldn't that work just as well?

Refers to notes

According to these notes you eat locusts and honey. Are you mad? Don't you realise you're going to alienate both the vegetarian and the dentistry lobbies? I'm a great one for a macrobiotic diet but people will think you're weird.

I think we need to work on your speeches. "Repent ye: for the Kingdom of Heaven is at hand." You must be crazy thinking you are going to get anywhere with a message about repentance. People don't want to hear that they've got to stop doing what they enjoy. It's just not 'on message'. We've got to put some spin on the whole "Repent ye" thing. It's too harsh. How about, "Think twice: the Kingdom of Heaven is a viable option"?

Think image John. Image. Image. Image. When your average man or woman in the desert looks at you do they see someone who makes them feel all warm and fuzzy inside? Do they see someone they'd like to invite into their homes and perhaps share some 'Chateau Shiloh' with? We want people to see the real you John but we want them to see the real John we want them to see and not be distracted by the real real John that we don't want them to see. Do you follow? Of course you do.

The trouble John is that you're not very popular with the people who matter. Common men or women may flock to see and hear you do your thing, but the movers and shakers who shape public opinion just aren't impressed.

If you listen to me John, I think we can turn public opinion around. I believe we can repackage you. Presentation is the key. Let's forget about the prophet thing and go for re-branding you as an entertainer. I'll arrange for you to attend some drama lessons. And what about dance? Another client of mine is having his daughter take some lessons.

It's been great chatting to you. I feel like we've really bonded. You just toddle off back to the wilderness and I'll launch our campaign. We'll do lunch sometime.

Jason's mobile phone rings.

Excuse me John, busy, busy, busy.

Answers phone.

Hello? Oh hi! Herod! I was just talking about you. I've met this absolutely wonderful prophet you simply must network with. You'll love him to pieces. I'll introduce you.

Barely glancing at John.

Ciao, John.

END

A Quick Word

Characters
Andrew
Sarah

Bible Background
'The first thing he did was to find his brother Simon.' John 1.35-42

On stage is Sarah, Peter's wife. She is in the process of preparing the evening meal. Enter Andrew, Peter's brother. He is slightly out of breath and obviously in a bit of a hurry.

Andrew   Oh hello, Sarah. Is Peter here? I'd like a quick word.

Sarah   No, I haven't seen hide nor hair of him since first thing this morning.

Andrew   Do you know where he is?

Sarah   I thought he was with you.

Andrew   He's not.

Sarah   Are you sure?

Andrew   *(Looking around and searching his pockets.)* Peter? Peter? No I can't seem to find him. Of course I'm sure he's not with me.

Sarah   Well, in that case, I haven't a clue.

Andrew   It's important.

Sarah   Have you tried the boat?

Andrew   Yes, I've just come from there.

Sarah   And he's not on board?

Andrew Sarah, the boat is twenty feet long and less than five feet wide. I think I'd have noticed a six foot fisherman.

Sarah I'm only trying to be helpful, Andrew.

Andrew I'm sorry.

Sarah He should be home soon, it's nearly time for his supper. Would you like to stay and eat with us? There's plenty. It's his favourite, Lamb Surprise.

Andrew What's the surprise?

Sarah It's made with fish.

Andrew Thank you, but I'm in a bit of a rush. Tell Peter I'm looking for him, will you, please.

Sarah Certainly. Can I give him a message?

Andrew The message is that I'm looking for him.

Sarah Yes, but why?

Andrew Oh, I want him to meet someone.

Sarah Who?

Andrew Jesus.

Sarah Oh, not that teacher from Nazareth?

Andrew You've heard of him?

Sarah Of course I've heard of him. You'd have to have been asleep these last few weeks not to have heard of him.

Andrew What have you heard about him?

Sarah	That he's a friend of that mad man, John. The one who eats locusts and ducks ...
Andrew	Ducks?
Sarah	Ducks people underwater. Baptism or something. Anyway he's very strange and any friend of his is bound to be very strange as well. Why do you want Peter to meet Jesus? Peter's strange enough already, thank you very much.
Andrew	I've spent some time with John recently. He's a great man.
Sarah	He's a weirdo you mean.
Andrew	He says that Jesus is the Messiah, the anointed one. I believe him and I want Peter to meet him. Look, when he gets here, tell him I want to see him and that I'll meet him on the beach. And why don't you come as well?
Sarah	Don't be silly. Why would I want to meet with a teacher? And why would my Peter? He's a working man, not an academic.
Andrew	Jesus is a working man. He's a carpenter and I've heard he's a good shepherd too. You'd like him.
Sarah	A shepherd? Do you think he might give Peter a job? It would be great if he could work part-time as a shepherd. Just think, I could cook Fish Surprise.
Andrew	As a matter of fact a job was mentioned. Jesus wants to make us fishers of men.
Sarah	What's the catch? I mean what use would Peter be to a holy man? Peter can be a bit coarse sometimes. We don't want him offending Jesus. After all, he won't be used to rough people. No offence Andrew, but your brother is not exactly the religious type.
Andrew	I don't think he's looking for religious types.

Sarah	Andrew, you don't have any great expectations do you?
Andrew	What do you mean?
Sarah	You don't think Jesus will change Peter?
Andrew	All I know is that if I don't take Peter to see him, we'll never find out. I owe him that.
Sarah	Who? Peter or Jesus?
Andrew	Both I suppose.
Sarah	Well, I don't suppose it'll do any harm. I'll tell Peter you are looking for him.
Andrew	On the beach.
Sarah	On the beach, right. That's where Jesus is, is it?
Andrew	That's where I left him, yes. He seems to like the water. He said he was thinking of going for a walk later.

END

Missing Friends

Characters
Sarah
Rachel

Bible Background
John 11. 1-44

Two women are talking at the reception after a funeral.

Sarah   It's tragic.

Rachel   He wasn't very old.

Sarah   No.

Rachel   What did he ... you know ... of?

Sarah   I don't know. It was quite sudden. One day he coughed, the next day he had a headache. A few days later he was ...

Rachel   Yes.

Sarah   I was shocked when I heard.

Rachel   I was devastated.

Sarah   I was shocked and devastated.

Rachel   Shocked, devastated and moved to tears.

Sarah   Me too.

Rachel   He was a nice man, Lazarus.

Sarah   Very nice.

Rachel   Mind you, the whole family is nice.

Sarah	Nice, yes.
Rachel	Well Martha is nice. Mary's a bit ...
Sarah	Strange. Yes. But she's got nice hair.
Rachel	Oh very nice hair, yes
Sarah	I do love a good funeral.
Rachel	So do I. You get to meet up with people you haven't seen in ages.
Sarah	Do you know everyone here?
Rachel	Not everyone, no. Who's that over there?
Sarah	Jesus from Nazareth. He's the Rabbi who conducted the service, remember?
Rachel	I'm afraid I missed the service. I was late. I wish the Romans would build one of their roads between here and the city. These shoes were never meant for the provinces. So that's this Jesus I've been hearing about.
Sarah	Yes. I understand he's an itinerant preacher.
Rachel	He looks a bit scruffy. You'd have thought he'd have dressed up for the occasion. Who are those other people?
Sarah	His followers. I expect they're just here for the buffet.
Rachel	Well the cheesy dip is just wonderful.
Sarah	They're certainly making short work of the hors d'oeuvres.
Rachel	And who's that over there, serving the punch?
Sarah	The deceased.
Rachel	Well, as I was saying, it's nice seeing people you haven't seen in ages. END

Palmed Off

Characters
Larry
Ruth
Mary

Bible Background
Mark 11.1-10

Larry is staffing a rather tacky souvenir stall. It stocks t-shirts, mugs, and palm leaves.

Larry   Hosanna! Hosanna in the highest! Get yer, 'Hosanna in the highest', T-shirts here! Come on ladies and gentlemen! Get yer high-class quality souvenirs! Get yer, 'I've seen the Messiah', T-shirts! Take home a momento of this momentous occasion!

Enter Ruth and Mary carrying deck chairs and a picnic.

Ruth   I didn't realise there would be so many people.

Mary   No.

Ruth   I thought we'd just set ourselves down by the side of the road and have our picnic as the procession passed by.

Mary   Yes.

Ruth   But we're not going to get anywhere near the roadside, are we? Not with that crowd.

Mary   I did say we should have set out earlier.

Ruth   Well I didn't know the whole city was going to turn out, did I?

Mary   Royalty always draws a big crowd. He is supposed to be a king.

Ruth	King of the Jews, Saviour, Messiah; you name it, he's it. Apparently he's going to sweep majestically in to the city and roast the Romans.
Mary	Rout dear. Rout the Romans.
Ruth	Whatever. Look, up there. On that hillock. We should be able to see from up there.

They climb up and set their deck chairs near to Larry's stall.

Mary	Oh yes, I can see quite well. Just look at all those people.
Ruth	What are they all holding?
Mary	Palm leaves, I think.
Ruth	I wonder where they got them from? Somebody has stripped all the trees bare.
Larry	Palm leaves! Get yer palm leaves here. Get yer lovely palm leaves here.

Larry waves a palm leaf.

Mary	I think we should. It'll be nice to have something to remember the occasion by.

They go over to the stall.

Ruth	How much are the palm leaves?
Larry	Two shekels each.
Ruth	Two! That's an awful lot.
Larry	Well, as you so correctly observed somebody has nicked 'em from all the local trees.
Mary	There must be some growing locally.

31

Larry	Not for at least seven miles.
Mary	How do you know?
	Larry holds up a saw.
Larry	Call it a hunch.
Mary	Oh ...
Ruth	What else have you got?
Larry	I've got T-shirts bearing the slogans, 'Hosanna in the highest', and 'I've seen the Messiah'. And I've also got these, 'I heart Galilee' mugs.
Ruth	Very nice.
Mary	Tasteful.
Larry	Good taste is my middle name.
Ruth	*(Looking towards the road)* Something's happening.
Mary	He must be coming.
Larry	Oh no!
Mary	What's wrong?
Larry	I've still got all this merchandise to flog. If I don't shift it today I'll be stuck with it.
Mary	Why?
Larry	Face it love, this Jesus may be a wonderful person, but messiahs come and messiahs go but a profit margin is here forever.

Ruth	There he is!

Ruth and Mary wave and shout.

Mary	Cooee! Cooeee, Mr Messiah.
Ruth	Alleluia!
Larry	Long live the king!

They stop waving.

Ruth	Well that was very nice.
Mary	I love a parade.
Larry	Lovely, but what am I going to do with this left-over stock?
Mary	Can't you use it next time?
Larry	No, there won't be a next time. This Jesus is just a fad you see. In ten years time no-one will even remember his name.
Ruth	So, what are you going to do?
Larry	In my line of work you have to anticipate the future and always be one step ahead of the crowd.
Mary	Come on Ruth, let's go home.
Ruth	Just coming, dear.
Larry	*(Shouting)* T-Shirts! Get yer T-Shirts! Get yer, 'FREE BARABBAS', T-Shirts here!

END

Where There's a Will ...

Characters
Son
Dad
Narrator
Friend

Bible Background
Luke 15. 11-32

Son rushes on stage, followed closely by Dad.

Narrator There was once a man who had two sons.
One day, one of the sons went to his father and said ...

Son Hi Dad, how are you feeling?

Dad Fine! Never felt better.

Son Oh! So you're not even a teensy-weensy bit ill then?

Dad No.

Son No sharp pains in the chest?

Dad No.

Son No agonising twinges in the head?

Dad No.

Son Oh! So you're not about to die then?

Dad No! Why ... do you want me to?

Son No! No! Of course not. Well ... not unless you feel like it.

Dad   Feel like it! What, dying?

Son   Anytime in the next few minutes would be fine.

Dad   Look, let me get this straight ... you want me dead?

Son   It's nothing personal!

Dad   It is! You come to me, out of the blue, and wish me dead. Why?

Son   I'm broke! I need my part of the inheritance.

Dad   Have you been reading my will?

Son   Well ... I caught a glimpse of it ... lying around in your study.

Dad   In my safe!?

Son   Which was blown open by a gust of wind as I was passing.

Dad   Safes do have a habit of doing that, don't they?

Narr.   Greatly saddened by his son's request, the father divided his estate into two.

Dad   *(Dad mimes tearing paper in half, giving it to Son.)* Here's your bit.

Dad exits.

Son   Ta, Dad! It's been nice knowing you.

Narr.   Evidently! And off he set, to a foreign land ...

Enter Friend.

Where he spent his money on wine ...

Son and Friend mime picking up glasses of wine and sipping.

… song … and wild women.

Son   I need a wild, wild woman!

Son, realising that acting is not such a bad job after all, makes straight for the most attractive female that he has so far spotted in the audience, and sits on her lap.

Hi, my name's Prodigal, what's yours?

Narr.   Until at last the money ran out …

Son mimes empty wine glass, returns to stage.

and all his friends left him …

Friend turns his back on Son who looks suitably rejected.

Then a severe famine hit the land.

Friend drops bucket marked 'Severe Famine' on ground in front of Son who looks puzzled.

Soon the Son was starving.

Son   Ooh, I'm peckish.

Narr.   Starving!

Son   Ooh, I'm hungry.

Narr.   Starving!

Son   All right. I'm starving!

Narr.   In desperation, he attached himself to a local landowner.

Friend   (*He puts on farmer's hat.*) Ooh arrr!

Narr.   Who set him to work feeding the pigs.

Son   Pigs?

Narr.   Pigs!

Friend becomes a pig and makes suitable pig noises.

Son   Pigs! Are you sure they're Kosher?

Son picks up 'Severe Famine' bucket and begins to feed pig.

Narr.   Soon, even the food the pigs ate began to look tempting ...

Son attempts to steal back some of the pig's food. The pig snorts with displeasure.

Suddenly, the Son had an idea.

Son mimes an electric light bulb appearing over head.

Son   Ping! I have an idea! Even the lowest of my father's servants have a better life than this. I will go back to him, and throw myself at his mercy. "Father," I shall say, "forgive the great wrong I've done you. I've sinned against God, and against you. Have mercy on me, I beg."

Narr.   And off he set ...

Son launches himself off the stage and embarks on an epic journey through the audience. Suitable epic music is provided - Mussorgsky's 'Night on a Bare Mountain' is good.

Exit Friend. Dad enters.

Narr.   Meanwhile ... *(Son carries on epic journey)* Meanwhile ... *(There's no stopping the Son)* MEANWHILE !

Son stops in his tracks and realises that the whole audience is watching him.

Son   Sorry.

Narrator exits.

Dad   Oh! What a cruel, cruel world this is. Every day I search the horizon, looking for my boy.

Son tries to attract Dad's attention from audience.

My Boy!

Son   Daddy!

Son rushes on stage embraces Dad and swings him round. Dad tries to do the same but Son is too heavy. Son falls to Dad's knees and clutches his leg.

Father, forgive the great wrong I have done you. I have sinned against God, and against you, have mercy on me I beg.

Dad   OK.

Son   *(Beating head against Dad's leg)* No, please, please hear me, please!

Dad   OK!

Son   OK? What, no stern lecture on moral fibre? No long list of Do's and Don'ts? No, "If you ever step out of line again, I'll flay you alive!", type talks? Daddy !

Son leaps into Dad's arms.

Dad   Kill the fatted calf! Let's have a party!

Dad drops Son on floor.

Son	No! ... No, I must work for you, in the field.
Dad	But I don't need another servant, I want my son back.
Son	Good point. Let's have a party!
Son & Dad	*(Singing)* Aga. do,do,do, push pineapple, shake the tree ... (etc.)

END

Body Matters

Characters
Polly
Official

Bible Background
1 Corinthians 12. 12-26

Official   Yes, Miss?

Polly   I've come to join the body of Christ.

Official   I see.

Polly   I thought I'd make an excellent eye.

Official   An eye.

Polly   You see I'm brilliant at watching people and so if anyone's misbehaving I'll spot them straight away and alert the foot.

Official   The foot, Miss?

Polly   So it can give the sinner a hard kick.

Official   I'm afraid that my records show that we already have the requisite number of eyes.

Polly   Oh. In that case I'll be a hand. That way I can point to anyone who's falling short of the mark and if necessary give them a sharp poke.

Official   The hands that we are currently using are managing very well and we are unlikely to change them in the foreseeable future. Sorry.

Polly   How about the tongue? I could be used to denounce sin and demand repentance.

Official   If you don't mind me saying Miss, I think you may have a mistaken impression of what it means to be part of the body of Christ.

Polly   I could be a tooth. I'm pretty sharp.

Official   The eyes are for vision and for seeing the way ahead.

Polly   An elbow then. I'm flexible.

Official   The feet are for balance and for moving forward.

Polly   How about an ear? I can be very attentive.

Official   And the tongue is for instruction and communication.

Polly   I'd make a brilliant eyebrow. I can do startled. I can do sad. Angry. Quizzical.

Official   We have a vacancy in the shoulder department.

Polly   What about lips? Smile. Scowl. Sneer.

Official   The shoulders need people to bear loads and to put against the wheel.

Polly   It doesn't sound very glamorous. Couldn't someone else be a shoulder? I don't want to be leaned on.

Official   Why not?

Polly   It doesn't matter.

Official   Yes it does.

Polly   No it doesn't.

Official   It does.

Polly   Doesn't.

Official   Does.

Polly	Doesn't.
Official	Does.
Polly	Doesn't.
Official	Doesn't.
Polly	Does ... oops.
Official	Well? Why don't you want to be leaned on?
Polly	I'm only little. I might get crushed.
Official	I see. And what's the real reason?
Polly	*(Muttering)* I'm afraid I might let someone down.
Official	Pardon?
Polly	*(Shouting)* I'M AFRAID I MIGHT LET SOMEONE DOWN!
Official	Ah, I understand. You're scared of failure. You're scared of being a dud.
Polly	Yes.
Official	A turkey.
Polly	Yes.
Official	A flop.
Polly	Right.
Official	A debacle, a fiasco, an unmitigated disaster.
Polly	Alright, alright, that's enough. Don't rub it in. I'll go quietly.
Official	Go where?

Polly	Over there to shiver on my own.
Official	Shiver?
Polly	I'm a cold shoulder.
Official	I wish you wouldn't go.
Polly	Tough.
Official	I beg your pardon?
Polly	I'm being a hard shoulder now.
Official	Please, you're upsetting me.
Polly	Don't worry. I'll be your shoulder to cry on.
Official	Then don't be afraid if people lean on you because you're a shoulder in the body of Christ.
Polly	Are you sure?
Official	I'm sure. You see you've got the rest of the body supporting you.
Polly	And it doesn't matter what part of the body we are because we all have a role to play.
Official	That's right.
Polly	Okay then. I'd be proud to be a shoulder in the body of Christ. At least it comes with it's own accommodation.
Official	I don't understand.
Polly	Haven't you ever heard of a shoulder pad? Come on, I'm having a party.

END

Supermin

Characters
John
Sean

Bible Background
'Are they men of unimpeachable character?' Titus 1. 5-9
1 Timothy 5. 17-18

*Adjust to correspond with particular denomination or cut as necessary.

John   And it came to pass that the people called Methodist* didst say unto themselves ...

Sean   We must appoint ourselves a new leader.

John   We shall give this person great power and responsibility and of the conference* he shall be president.*

Sean   But in case he actually wants to do anything with this power and responsibility we shall only appoint him for one year.*

John   It should take him that long just to read the job specification manual.

Sean   Then the people called Methodist* didst turn to themselves and say ...

John   Let us also appoint leaders for our churches. We shall call them Ministers* for they shall minister unto us as angels do.

Sean   Yea verily, they will be most perfect whether they be male or female.

John   They shall preach sermons unto us which are full of wisdom but are never dull.

Sean   Sermons that speak to the very young and to the very old.

John   And sermons that speak to the elderly lady who does not wear a hearing aid but who still sitteth at the back.

Sean   And the people said Amen.

John   And the people said let him run youth groups and mother and toddler groups.

Sean   And let her conduct all age worship with nothing but a guitar and a glove puppet for protection.

John   He shall sing songs about wriggly worms and fuzzy wuzzy bears.

Sean   And he shall even do the movements.

John   He shall visit the sick in hospital and in their homes.

Sean   But he shall never be too sick himself to chair that all important committee on raising funds for the purchase of new hymn books.

John   And the people will visit him in his home at any hour of the day or of the night. But most especially at meal times.

Sean   Let him wear the efforts of the Knit and Sew group with good grace.

John   Even though the jumper be pink and a bit short and the balaclava mauve and a bit tight.

Sean   Let her be a postman for the Lord and deliver leaflets and Christmas cards and donation envelopes - and on rare occasions pizza menus by mistake.

John   He shall open the Christmas fete and he will wear the Santa costume.

Sean	She shall bring new members to the church but not alienate the old members.
John	She will drink church tea and church coffee until her taste buds are destroyed.
Sean	He will live in a house called a Manse* which was last decorated in nineteen seventy-three.
John	And if he complains about the howling draft he will be told that fresh air is good for him and that there is no budget for repairs.
Sean	And the property committee said Amen.
John	She will always be tactful and never laugh when she baptises a child as Elvis or Madonna.
Sean	He will be called upon to judge the Guild* Cakemaking Competition and he will have to taste them all.
John	Yea, even the one that is flavoured with Marmite and broccoli.
Sean	And it shall be said of the Minister* that she knoweth all things.
John	Including, the meaning of life and the whereabouts of the overhead projector bulbs.
Sean	And it shall pass that many people will tell him that he is not like his predecessor who was a most excellent Minister*.
John	Yea, most verily the former Minister* was a most virtuous man who did not mind that he had a circuit* of seventeen churches in an area of over one hundred square miles because he was a REAL man of God.
Sean	And the people shall say what a pity it was that he had that breakdown.

John	And then the people called Methodist* didst say unto themselves ...
Sean	Perhaps we do expect too much of our Ministers*.
John	But then they did look to each other and laugh saying:
Sean	No, of course we do not. They have been to college haven't they?
John	Then in churches across the land Ministers* did stand in their pulpits or on their platforms and look at their new congregations and say unto themselves ...
Sean	Perhaps this time it will be different.
John	And the people smiled encouragingly as they announced the first hymn.
John & Sean	Amen.

END

Onward Christian Soldiers

Characters
Two Soldiers

Bible Background
Ephesians 6. 10-20

Enter two soldiers. One a Lieutenant, the other a Private. They are both singing.

Both　　*(Singing)*
Onward Christian soldiers
Marching as to war
With the cross of Jesus
Going on before.

Lieut.　　Alright, you can stop singing now.

Private　*(Still singing)*
Christ the royal master
Leads against the foe.

Lieut.　　Yes, yes. That'll do.

Private　*(Still singing)*
Forward into battle
See! His banners go.
Onward Christian ...

Lieut.　　Oh, do be quiet.

Private　*(Still singing)*
... soldiers
Marching as to war.

Lieut.　　Oh I know. Ten-shun! *(The Private snaps to attention.)*

Private　Private Nicely, reporting for Christian duty, Sir!

Lieut.	Jolly good, jolly good. Well, as your commanding officer, all that is left for me to do is wish you well in your new life and to send you on your way. Any questions?
Private	Yes Sir. Quite a few, Sir.
Lieut.	Oh dear me. Well you'd better fire away, Private ... Er ... Private ...
Private	Nicely, Sir.
Lieut.	Nicely, yes. Well, go ahead.
Private	Well, Sir, you know when you sign up to be a Christian soldier?
Lieut.	Yes.
Private	You think it's going to be full of excitement. You know, doing good and righting wrongs.
Lieut.	Doing good and righting wrongs? It's the Church you've joined, not Robin Hood's band of merry men.
Private	Yes, but I thought being a Christian was all about taking risks.
Lieut.	Taking risks? Whatever gave you that idea?
Private	The Bible did, Sir. It's full of stories about people doing risky things while they are serving God.
Lieut.	Oh yes?
Private	Saint Paul was shipwrecked. Peter was thrown in prison. Stephen was stoned to death. That kind of thing only happens if you're living a pretty risky kind of life.
Lieut.	And you don't think that Christians have a risky lifestyle today, do you soldier?

Private	No Sir.
Lieut.	Well let me tell you, sunny Jim, that I live my Christian life on the edge.
Private	Really Sir?
Lieut.	Oh yes. Every Sunday I have to decide whether to sit at the back of the church or at the front. I have to decide whether to drink the coffee or play safe with the tea.
Private	But what about fighting injustice and speaking out for the voiceless? What about feeding the hungry and healing the sick?
Lieut.	And every week I have to decide how much to put on the collection plate.
Private	But Sir, I joined up to build the Kingdom. To make a difference.
Lieut.	Make a difference? Listen, without me we'd still be using the 'Sacred Songs and Solos'.
Private	Surely there has to be more to the Christian life than what goes on inside the church.
Lieut.	That will do, Nicely. What goes on inside the church is very important. How the seating is set out. Where to place the overhead projector screen. Whether the praise band is properly miked up or not. You think that these things just happen? Well they don't you know. They take planning. They take commitment. They take a large numbers of committees.
Private	Wouldn't it be a better strategy to get out in the world and declare what we believe?
Lieut.	The drawback with that particular modus operandi is that the world would then know where we are.

Private   But isn't that exactly what we want? Aren't we suppose to be like a city on a hill. We must not hide our light under a bushel.

Lieut.   Which is exactly why we're going to have a special day of outreach just as soon as we've organised a working party to discuss the processes needed to form a steering committee for a group to formally set out the criteria by which such a day might be considered in the nearish future.

Private   So we're not actually going to do anything. Not in the everyday sense of the word. We're just going to stay safely inside our church.

Lieut.   It's what we've done for centuries, Private.

Private   I suppose it is safer.

Lieut.   Much safer.

Private   And I suppose that if we're not the ones out there making a difference someone else is bound to do the job instead.

Lieut.   Bound to.

Private   I wonder who it will be?

Both   Onward Christian soldiers
Eyes fixed on the floor
We keep our lives so busy
We don't have time for more.
Oh! Sing our songs of praises
Turn our heads away
With our holy phrases
They won't know what we say.

Onward Christian soldiers
Marching as before
Our thoughts on affectations
Rather than the law.

We should stand for justice
We should call for peace
Instead we stand for coffee
Will wonders never cease.
We look away from suffering
Turn away from pain
Then sing another chorus
Proclaiming our God reigns.

Onward Christian soldiers
Locked inside the church
You're called to make a difference
Not leave them in the lurch.

Lieut. About turn!

Both soldiers turn around and march out.

END

The Prayer Emporium

Characters
Beverly
Customer

Bible Backround
Matthew 6.1, 5-13

A customer enters a store. Beverly is behind the counter.

Beverly   Welcome to the Prayer Emporium. My name is Beverly. How may I be of assistance?

Cust.   I'd like to buy a prayer.

Beverly   Certainly, Madam. And may I enquire of you the exact nature of the prayer you are wishing to purchase?

Cust.   I'm not exactly sure. I've never really had much to do with prayers before.

Beverly   Lovely. Then it will be my pleasure to guide you through our comprehensive range of prayers that we have on offer. Would that be agreeable to you?

Cust.   Certainly.

Beverly   Lovely. Now, right at the top end of the market we have our 'Classic' range. These are deluxe prayers that have endured over the centuries. For example, we have here the 'Kyrie Eleison', the 'Sursum Corda', the 'Sanctus', and, of course, the ever popular 'Nunc Dimittis'.

Cust.   They sound beautiful. What do they mean?

Beverly   I am afraid I am unable to supply you with that information on account of the fact that I don't myself know. However, I am able to assure you that when said in a beautiful sing-song way

53

they sound lovely. Moving on, we have the famous 'Paternoster'. Now I am conversant with the meaning of this one on account of the fact that we used to do it at school. It means 'Our Father'.

Cust. I think I've heard of it.

Beverly It's very popular because it reminds people of school and Sunday School or the kiddy's christening. You can recite it a bit like a nursery rhyme. 'Our Father, who art in Heaven, Hallowed be thy name', and so on.

Cust. Yes, but does it mean anything?

Beverly I expect it does, yes.

Cust. What?

Beverly Pardon?

Cust. What does it mean?

Beverly Lovely ... Moving on we have prayers of intercession, prayers of supplication, prayers of imprecation. We have invocation, benediction, commination and devotion. Also petitionary prayers, mitigating prayers and contemplative prayers.

Cust. They all sound a bit formal.

Beverly Oh you want casual prayers.

Cust. Do I?

Beverly We have a full range; for all occasions. For example, we have prayers asking for forgiveness for all things ranging from accidentally bumping your car into your neighbour's gate post to deliberately hiding the television remote control to annoy your husband.

Cust. They sound useful.

Beverly Oh, they are. We also do a full range of dead pet prayers for cats, dogs, rabbits, gerbils and hamsters. The goldfish one even comes with precise instructions on when to flush.

Cust. I don't think they'd be appropriate.

Beverly Well, what about our emergency prayers.

Cust. What are they?

Beverly Well, for all sorts of emergencies really. You use them when your brakes fail or your parachute doesn't open. You should read the warning on the label though.

Cust. What does it say?

Beverly Sudden prayers make God jump.

Cust. I'm not sure. I've been invited to a prayer meeting you see. It's at my local church. I don't want to get there and appear to be the odd one out because I don't know what I'm doing.

Beverly Oh, why didn't you say? I've got just the thing. It's an assortment of sounds.

She takes out a cloth bag.

Cust. How do they work?

Beverly Whenever there's an awkward pause you just select one and use it.

Cust. Can I hear some?

Beverly dips into the bag.

Beverly Hmmm. Yes Lord. Alleluia. Hmm.

Cust. They sound ideal. Can I try?

Beverly   Certainly.

The customer dips into the bag.

Cust.   Praise him. Yes. Amen. Hmm. Thank you.

Beverly   Well done. You've got the hang of them straight away.

Cust.   I'll take a selection, please.

Beverly   Lovely. Will there be anything else?

Cust.   No thank you. Though I must say I'm rather disappointed.

Beverly   And why might that be, Madam?

Cust.   Well, I did think that I might actually get to talk to God when I prayed.

Beverly   Oh no, Madam. Christians have spent centuries finding ways to avoid doing that. It's a pity really, he's so interesting when you get to know him.

Cust.   Do you pray then?

Beverly   No. I just chat to him like he's a friend. And do you know what?

Cust.   No?

Beverly   He doesn't seem to mind a bit. Next please.

END

Suffer The Children

Characters
Sunday School Teacher

Bible Background
Mark 10. 13-16

A stand-in Sunday School teacher addresses her class of very young children.

Teacher   All right children, it's time to stop what we are doing and listen to me. That's right, stop colouring in your Amazing Technicolour Dream Coats and come and sit on the mat. Michael, you as well dear. Come along, hip-hop mister Bunny.

Are we all sitting nicely? We're going to talk to God.

Nigel, God would like it a lot better if you faced this way when you talk with him. Yes, I know God can see you wherever you look, but right now his attention is over here.

Stop poking Daniel, Margaret. It's not nice. No, I don't think he does like it. Oh, you do, Daniel. Well, I don't, so stop it.

Right, we're going to talk to God about what we've been doing this morning. What have we been doing this morning? Colouring in, yes. Having stories, yes. What was the story about? Do you remember? It was about Easter. And what happened at Easter? Jesus died, yes. Yes, it was sad. Your cat died, did he, Amanda. Well, that was sad as well. But I expect he was very old, wasn't he? He was very poorly then. No? He was run over. No, Jesus wasn't run over.

Do you remember what happened on Easter day? You got some chocolate eggs did you? That was nice. But what happened to Jesus? No, he didn't get any eggs. Something wonderful happened. No, the Easter Bunny didn't come. Jesus rose again. Do you remember?

He died to set us free. You're three. And you're four. You're three and a half, are you? That's nice. No, Jesus died to set us free from feeling sad about our sins. I'm sorry, Michael, what did you say? Fish have sins. Do they? They help them to swim? Oh! Fish have fins, Michael. They're not quite the same.

Oh, dear, we've strayed a little from our path. We were going to pray to God, weren't we? Yes. Let's find out who needs our prayers today. Let's ask Mr Prayer Bear.

She takes out a teddy bear and holds it up.

(Gruffly) Hello children. Who do you want to pray for today?

(Normal voice) No I haven't got a sore throat. That was Mr Prayer Bear talking. You could see my lips moving. Yes it was me talking. Mr Prayer Bear can't really talk. Yes it is rather silly isn't it.

She puts the bear down hurriedly.

Who do we know who needs our prayers? You've got a brown crayon have you. And you're moving house are you, Michael? How exciting. We will miss you. Oh, you'll still be able to come to Sunday School here, will you? Oh good.

Yes, Stephanie? Well you know where it is. Hurry back.

Well I know we'd all like to pray for Mrs Tomplinson, your normal Sunday School teacher. Let's pray that she recovers from her little breakdown and comes back to us soon. Very soon. I know that Mrs Tomplinson would like to thank God for the invention of Prozac.

Now, is there anything else we want to thank God for? Baked beans. Yes we can thank him for those. Spaghetti hoops, yes. Fish fingers. Shall we just thank God for all the lovely food he gives us to eat?

All right then. Hands together and eyes closed. Do you remember why we close our eyes and put our hands together? Yes, to stop us hitting people while we pray. No God doesn't like it. Yes I know you could do a karate chop but that wouldn't be nice.

Hands together, eyes closed, head bowed ... Are you all right, Alison? Why are you crying? Oh, I am sorry your Daddy isn't very well. You're a bit frightened are you? Yes I know Jesus would like you to tell him all about it. He loves your Daddy as much as you do. We'll all ask Jesus to help your Daddy.

Hands together, eyes closed, head bowed ... I can still see you, Michael.

END

Christian Drama from Nimbus Press

Various authors

Platform Souls – Gospel Sketches for the New Millennium
Sketches for Seeker Services 1 – for the unchurched and new Christians
Sketches for Seeker Services 2
Celebrating Light – Sketches for Churches

Edward Bennett

Lets Go to Bethlehem, Full House in Bethlehem,
Good News in Bethlehem – Christmas plays
The Rose Has Thorns – A play for Easter

Stephen Deal

Making Waves – The Quick Sketch Collection
Kingdom Airways – The Quick Sketch Collection

Les Ellison

First Easter – Nine Holy Week Dramas

Rosi MorganBarry

Angel's Counsel – A True Christmas 'Fairytale'

Ronald Rich

Even More Surprise Sketches
Time to Speak – A play about Peter and Pilate 30 years on

Clifford Sharp / Jonathan Curnow

The Golden Age – An Environmental play
The Price of Olives – A play about Jesus' family life
My Kind of God - 2 short plays
Is This your Life & the Pearl of Great Price
The Good Church Guide – Who's the best?
Looking for a King – 2 new short Christmas plays

Christian Humour

It happened to a Christian ... True funny and sad stories

Reg Frary

Heavenly Choirs ... and others, Don't upset the choir, Meanwhile Back at the
Vestry, Have you heard our Choir. – amusing stories from the choir vestry!